Animal Attacks

# SNAKE ATTACK

by Lisa Owings

BELLWETHER MEDIA · MINNEAPOLIS, MN

# TORQUE

Are you ready to take it to the extreme? Torque books thrust you into the action-packed world of sports, vehicles, mystery, and adventure. These books may include dirt, smoke, fire, and dangerous stunts. WARNING : read at your own risk.

Library of Congress Cataloging-in-Publication Data

Owings, Lisa.
 Snake attack / by Lisa Owings.
     p. cm. -- (Torque: animal attacks)
 Includes bibliographical references and index.
 Summary: "Engaging images illustrate true snake attack stories and accompany survival tips. The combination of high-interest subject matter and light text is intended for students in grades 3 through 7"
--Provided by publisher.
 ISBN 978-1-60014-791-3 (hardcover : alk. paper)
 ISBN 978-1-60014-846-0 (paperback : alk. paper)
 1.  Snake attacks--Juvenile literature. 2.  Snakes--Behavior--Juvenile literature.  I. Title.
 QL666.O6O95 2013
 597.9615'3--dc23

                                       2012011216

Printed in the United States of America, North Mankato, MN.

A special thanks to Brian Cassey for contributing an image.

# TABLE OF CONTENTS

# Silent Strikers

Snakes are some of the most feared animals in the world. The most dangerous snakes strike quickly with needle-sharp **fangs**. These curved teeth drip **venom** that can kill within minutes. Fangs also help venomous snakes grasp struggling **prey**. **Constrictors** use a death grip on their **victims**. They wrap their bodies around prey and then slowly **strangle** them.

## Open Wide

Snakes can open their jaws wide to devour prey much larger than their heads. Some large snakes can swallow pigs or deer whole!

# Very Venomous

- **Beaked sea snake** (off the coasts of Africa, Asia, Australia, and New Guinea)

- **Black mamba** (Africa)

- **Boomslang** (Africa)

- **Cobra** (Africa, Asia)

- **Death adder** (Australia, New Guinea)

- **Eastern brown snake** (Australia, New Guinea)

- **Krait** (Asia)

- **Russell's viper** (Asia)

- **Taipan** (Australia, New Guinea)

- **Tiger snake** (Australia)

# Cheating Death

Danie Pienaar had spent the morning following rhinos through South Africa's Kruger National Park. By noon, he had reached the edge of a stream. Tall grasses brushed his bare legs. Suddenly Danie was startled by a flash of brown scales. It was a black mamba! He thought he had escaped its deadly bite. Then he saw his leg.

## Death Sentence

Black mamba venom is powerful enough to kill a person within 20 minutes. Without antivenom, a black mamba bite is often a death sentence.

Danie's whole body began to tingle. The venom was spreading. He was far from help and had limited supplies, but he would not give up. Thoughts of his family kept him going. He tied his belt tightly above the wound to slow the venom. Then he started hiking toward his truck. Walking grew harder with every step. His muscles began to shut down.

"I forced myself to walk and breathe slowly to try and slow my heartbeat down."

—Danie Pienaar

Danie stumbled into his truck. His **numb** legs and blurred vision made his driving wild. He nearly crashed into another vehicle. The people in the other car saw that he needed help. They rushed Danie to the hospital. Danie told the doctors in slurred speech what had happened. Then he passed out. When Danie woke up, he could not move. But he was alive.

Venomous Snakebite
## Symptoms

- **bad taste in mouth**
- **burning sensation**
- **swelling**
- **blistering**
- **vomiting**
- **dizziness**
- **blurred vision**
- **tingling or loss of feeling**
- **difficulty breathing**

## Fearless Return

Danie made a full recovery and returned to work at Kruger National Park. He even encountered a black mamba on his first day back!

# All Wrapped Up

It was a night like any other. Rachael Sullivan was playing catch with her sons outside their home in northern Australia. When the ball went rolling away, her two-year-old son Kye chased after it. That is when Rachael heard a terrible scream. Kye was in the grip of a 13-foot (4-meter) scrub python!

"Kye let out that horrible scream where you know something is very, very wrong."

—Rachael Sullivan

13

"A snake wouldn't know
the difference between
a two-year-old boy and
a wallaby."
—Dr. Rod Gilbert, veterinarian

Blood flowed from Kye's leg where the python's jaws held him. The huge snake was wrapped around Kye's small body. Its **coils** tightened around his ribs. Rachael tried to pull the snake off her son. But the python would not give up its meal.

## Super Squeezer

The reticulated python is the longest snake in the world. It can grow to be more than 30 feet (9 meters) long. It can also weigh more than 250 pounds (110 kilograms).

Neighbors Scott Tunnie and Xena Reeves heard Rachael's screams. Scott grabbed the python's head and started pulling. He unwound the python from Kye's wounded leg. Then the snake slithered up Scott's arm and began to squeeze.

Xena helped Scott battle the snake. She called the **paramedics**. It took two more neighbors to finally get the python under control. Kye was treated at a nearby hospital. He returned home the next day.

"Kye was really brave and just sat there with these big eyes while I bandaged his leg."

—Terese Cassidy, paramedic

## Forgiving Bitey

Kye waved good-bye to the python, which he named "Bitey," just days after the attack. The snake was released back into the wild.

Kye

# Prevent a Snake Attack

Snakes do not usually attack people unless they feel **threatened**. However, many people anger snakes by accident. Research snakes in your area and how to avoid them. Stay aware of your surroundings. Remember that some kinds of snakes live in trees and strike from above. Others wait underwater or hide beneath dirt or sand.

**Safety in Numbers**
Travel with other people in places where deadly snakes are common. A friend can run for help or treat your wounds if you are attacked.

Walking through tall grass is especially dangerous. Wear long pants and boots for protection. If you see a snake, give it plenty of space. Snakes often attack when they feel trapped.

# Survive a Snake Attack

Get medical help immediately if a snake bites you. Stay calm and still to slow down your heart rate. This slows the spread of venom. Wrap a bandage firmly around the wound. Try to remember what the snake looks like. This information can help doctors treat you. It will also help you get the correct **antivenom** faster.

If a constrictor attacks you, do anything you can to escape its deadly grip. Pull it by the tail if it starts to wrap around you. Keep your wits about you and you could survive a snake attack!

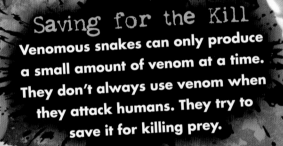

## Saving for the Kill

Venomous snakes can only produce a small amount of venom at a time. They don't always use venom when they attack humans. They try to save it for killing prey.

# Snake Attack Don'ts

- **NEVER** cut open the wound. This can cause an infection.

- **NEVER** try to suck out the venom. This just gives the venom another way into your body.

- **NEVER** try to catch or kill the snake. A severely injured snake can still attack you!

# Glossary

**antivenom**—a medicine that weakens venom; antivenom is given to victims of venomous bites.

**coils**—loops; constrictors use their bodies to form coils around their prey.

**constrictors**—snakes that wrap around and squeeze their prey; constrictors are not venomous.

**fangs**—sharp, curved teeth; some snakes have hollow fangs through which venom can move into a bite.

**numb**—unable to feel anything

**paramedics**—people who are trained to give emergency medical treatment

**prey**—animals that are hunted by other animals for food

**strangle**—to choke, or cut off one's air supply

**threatened**—likely to be in danger

**venom**—a poison that some snakes produce to kill prey or cause prey to stop moving

**victims**—people or animals that are hurt, killed, or made to suffer

# To Learn More

## AT THE LIBRARY

Buchholz, Rachel. *How to Survive Anything*. Washington, D.C.: National Geographic, 2011.

Owings, Lisa. *The King Cobra*. Minneapolis, Minn.: Bellwether Media, 2012.

Sexton, Colleen A. *Mambas*. Minneapolis, Minn.: Bellwether Media, 2010.

## ON THE WEB

Learning more about snakes is as easy as 1, 2, 3.

1. Go to www.factsurfer.com.

2. Enter "snakes" into the search box.

3. Click the "Surf" button and you will see a list of related Web sites.

With factsurfer.com, finding more information is just a click away.

# Index